STEPHEN
FOSTER
HIS LIFE

OTHER BOOKS

BY

CATHERINE OWENS PEARE

ALBERT EINSTEIN

MAHATMA GANDHI

STEPHEN

FOSTER

HIS LIFE

by
CATHERINE OWENS PEARE

illustrated by
MARGARET AYER

HOLT, RINEHART AND WINSTON
NEW YORK · CHICAGO · SAN FRANCISCO

Library of Congress Catalog Card Number: 52–9037

Published, September, 1952
Second Printing, September, 1954
Third Printing, November, 1958
Fourth Printing, September, 1963
Fifth Printing, April, 1966

96961-2313

Printed in the United States of America

CONTENTS

THE FOURTH OF JULY

CHAPTER

1

IT WAS THE FOURTH of July. The Foster family—all but Mrs. Foster—and their friends were celebrating America's freedom, laughing and singing and telling stories, as they sat around pine tables under a great oak tree in "Foster's Spring."

"Oh, say can you see, by the dawn's early light," sang the happy crowd of people.

"Tell us about the Indians!" cried one of the Foster children, when the song was finished.

"Well," said Mr. Foster, "I can remember when it would have been too dangerous to sit in this grove without our guns, because Indians lurked in the woods nearby."

The Foster children all laughed at their father, for Pittsburgh, Pennsylvania, was safe in 1826.

What a lot of Foster children there were! There was Charlotte Susanna, aged sixteen; Ann Eliza, aged fourteen; Henry, aged ten; Henrietta, aged seven; Dunning, aged five; and Morrison, aged three. William, the adopted oldest brother, was grown and away working.

And there was another new baby expected at the house any minute! That was why Mrs. Foster didn't come to the grove this year.

"Stay down at the grove with your father," the Foster children had been told. "Don't dare come near the house with your noise."

"Let's sing 'Yankee Doodle,'" someone shouted, and they all started to sing again.

The Fosters and their friends were so busy singing that they didn't notice Lieve running down the hill from the house. She burst in on the party.

"Marse Foster, he's here!" she gasped all out of breath. "The new baby is here."

Everyone crowded around Lieve, the Negro girl, and clamored for more news.

"Is it a boy or a girl?"

"It's a boy!" announced Lieve, tossing her head so that the red ribbons on her pigtails flew about her ears like bumblebees.

"What's his name? What's his name?"

William Foster stood up tall and proud.

"His name," announced the father of the new baby, "is Stephen Collins Foster."

Lieve turned and ran all the way up the hill to

the house. So did the six Foster children and their father, with three-year-old Morrison last, because his legs were too short to keep up.

Lieve stopped to get her breath when she reached the front door. A new baby meant that she had a lot of work to do.

"Mah goodness!" she whispered to herself. "Can't stand much more excitement. Sun's too hot."

Inside and upstairs to the nursery she hurried.

Charlotte Susanna, Ann Eliza, Henry, Henrietta, and Dunning were ahead of her, crowding around the cradle. Morrison toddled in behind.

"Shoo! Go away! Don't touch the baby!" ordered Lieve.

"He's so tiny!"

"He'll grow!"

From then on Lieve's most important work was to take care of the baby Stephen. Every day she gave him his bath, rocked him, and sang songs to him.

Stephen, or Stephie, as his family called him, grew fast. Soon he was able to crawl around on the floor by himself. He listened to Lieve singing as she baked bread. He listened to the rustle, rustle of silk when his mother or sisters swooshed by in their long, full skirts.

Whenever anyone played the piano, he clapped

his hands and gurgled for joy.

"Stephie loves music," they all agreed.

They were glad, because everyone in the Foster family liked music.

Sister Ann Eliza practiced the piano every day, and when her lesson was done she picked up her guitar and sang. Two-year-old Stephie liked that, too, so one day Ann Eliza laid her guitar on the floor in front of Stephen.

"You play the guitar, Stephie. Let me hear you play."

He strummed his fingers across the strings, and when he heard the tones he laughed and said, "Ittly pizani; ittly pizani," meaning, "little piano."

In the evening Mr. and Mrs. Foster, Ann Eliza, Henry, Henrietta, even seven-year-old Dunning and five-year-old Morrison, gathered around the piano to sing. Sometimes Mother played for them, while Mr. Foster played his violin. Neighbors liked to drop in and visit with the musical Fosters.

People liked to drop in any time of day. When the Foster children heard trotting horses and carriage wheels approaching the house, they all ran to the door to see who was calling. Carriage wheels meant that there were ladies coming, friends of Mother's, wearing big feather plumes on their hats, shawls around their shoulders, and long skirts.

"How are the children?" one lady would ask.

"They're fine, all except Stephie," Mrs. Foster usually said. "He has another cold."

Stephie was sick much oftener than most children. He caught cold easily and he had a sore throat almost every winter. He had whooping cough when he was only four years old.

If the Foster children heard one horse trotting up the driveway and no carriage wheels, that was Father. He traveled around on horseback, especially when he went to the Pennsylvania legislature. Father was an important man in Pittsburgh.

Father would swing down from his saddle, hitch the horse to a post, and climb the front porch. Charlotte, Ann Eliza, Henry, Henrietta, Dunning, Morrison, and Stephie would push the door open and rush out.

"Hello, Father! Hello!"

Mr. Foster would hug all of his children, while Henry or Dunning seized his furry stovepipe hat and tried it on.

If Stephie didn't rush to the door with the other children, Father would ask: "Is Stephie sick again?"

In the warm weather Stephie was seldom ill. Then he could run out and play under the big locust tree in the yard. Or he could watch Lieve carry pails of frothy milk down to the spring house to cool.

Stephie loved Lieve, and on Sunday morning,

when she put on her bonnet and walked to the door, he ran after her and pleaded, "Take me with you, Lieve!"

He knew she was going to church. Lieve scooped him up in her arms and ran down the hill to the road. Of course, he could go to church with her!

Lieve went to the Negro church, and Stephie loved to hear the Negroes sing. He loved to hear them, because they made up new songs as they went along. They sang their prayers and sang of their troubles and their work, or of anything they wished. They were exciting as they swayed back and forth and sang louder and louder. One tall Negro would stand up and begin a new melody:

"Go down, Moses!"

The congregation would join in:

"Way down in Judah Land."

Stephie sat very still as he listened to the Negro music.

Negroes sang as they felt. They made their own music, and he could do it, too, he discovered. He could make up a song about anything that he wished. He could invent his own tunes and his own words just the way the Negroes did.

Trotting along at Lieve's side on the way home from church, Stephie hummed and sang.

"What you singin'?" asked Lieve.

"I made up a song, Lieve! Listen to me sing!"

EVERYTHING SINGS

CHAPTER
2

WHEN STEPHIE WAS SIX his father gave him a drum, so that he could join in the family music. Then Stephie really showed his talent. He marched around the house playing rat-a-tat-tat on the drum, until his elders held their hands over their ears. He stuck a big chicken feather in his hat and tied a bright scarf around his waist, and whistled "Old Lang Syne."

Nine-year-old Morrison marched around behind Stephie, and sometimes even eleven-year-old Dunning joined the parade. They made a clatter up and down stairs with Stephie whistling, "Should old acquaintance be forgot and never brought to mind?"

"Where did Stephie learn to whistle? Where did he learn 'Old Lang Syne'?" his elders wanted to know.

When Stephie whistled a strange tune, they would ask each other, "What song is that?"

"Oh, Stephie made that one up," Dunning or Morrison would explain.

"Stephie's head is full of tunes," said Henrietta.

Stephen Foster's head was so full of tunes that he could find music wherever he went. He could stand down by the roadway and watch horses and carriages trotting by. The horses' feet kept time like his sister's fingers on the piano keys.

Sometimes a covered wagon drawn by oxen went past at a slower pace. Many people were going West in those days to seek their fortunes. They put all of their belongings into big wagons with round canvas tops and went out to the wild and dangerous West where the government would give them free land.

The driver of the covered wagon stood up on the wagon tongue, holding the reins in his left hand. He cracked the whip over the oxen with his right, and the whip sang through the air, as the driver called out, "Oh, ho-haw!" to encourage the animals to pull faster.

"Oh, ho-haw!" called Stephen.

"Ho-ho-ho!" yelled the driver, and he sounded as though he were singing.

Stephen ran after the wagon to hear more. Maybe the driver would make another melody. The big wooden wheels, taller than Stephen, squeaked in their axles. The driver made a low tone, like the Negro singing, "Go down, Moses!" The squeaking wheels made a high tone, like Father's violin.

At night the boy with a head full of melody would listen to the whippoorwill making still another tune. Stephen found he could change melodies. If a tune went up: one, two, three; he could turn it around and sing it down: three, two, one. He could change the whippoorwill's song, and add more song to it, and then give the song words—any words he wished—the way they did in Lieve's church. Sometimes he fell asleep singing softly to himself. Stephen's world was full of music.

When the family went walking on Sunday afternoon, Stephen would beg: "Let's go down to the river and listen to the steamboats!"

So down to the river they would stroll, Stephie holding the hand of one of the grownups, to watch the boats. Whichever way they walked they could find a river, because Pittsburgh is between two rivers, the Allegheny that comes down from the north, and the Monongahela that drifts in from the east. The two rivers join at Pittsburgh and flow on together to make the Ohio River.

"Here comes a steamboat!" shouted the Foster children. "Let's wait and see its name."

The huge wheel on the side of the steamboat turned and churned the water into suds, as the boat

9

turned its bow into the dock, and its whistles shrilled to let everyone know it was there.

"Blow your whistle again!" cried Stephen as he jumped up and down.

Passengers coming to Pittsburgh walked down the gangplank and looked around for a horse and carriage. Workmen ran up the gangplank to help carry off the cargo. They were strong men with rippling muscles who sang as they handed out barrels of flour and sugar and bundles of cloth. Some of them were Negroes who laughed and showed their white teeth.

"Sing some more!" called Stephen.

"Singing is just for fun, Stephie," his father explained. "Those men must work. Everyone must work to earn a living."

"Oh, dear!" sighed Mrs. Foster, as the family strolled away from the dock. "What kind of work will Stephie do? He isn't very strong."

"Well, nobody earns a living playing a musical instrument or singing," said Mr. Foster.

Stephen was small for his age, too, his mother fussed.

But whether he was too frail or too small, he was old enough for school, and in the fall he would have to begin learning his letters.

Dunning and Morrison were already in school, and the other Fosters were too old. Ann Eliza and

Henrietta were talking about getting married. Henry, who was sixteen, was away learning to be a tanner. Brother William, who was so much older than all the others because he was adopted, was already an engineer.

Dunning and Morrison, eleven and eight, were Stephen's real companions, because they were the youngest. When they heard that Stephie could at last come to school with them they jumped for joy. On the first day of school they sat in class with their hands folded on their desks waiting for Mother to arrive with Stephie. Once in a while Morrison would turn his head and peek out of the window.

At last he saw his mother walking up the path to Mrs. Harvey's school, holding her parasol in one hand and leading Stephie with the other hand. Stephen was wearing a new jacket with seven brass buttons down the front.

Stephen's face wore a sad expression when his mother led him into the classroom and left him with Mrs. Harvey. He liked to dream and run free. In school, his mother had explained, he would have to sit very still and pay attention. He felt frightened as his mother disappeared out of the door.

He slid into the seat and looked around. The whole roomful of students was staring at him, and finding Morrison's face didn't help much, because Morrison was far away on the other side of the class.

"Stand up, Stephen," he heard Mrs. Harvey say. Stephen stood up.

"Hold your hands at your sides."

He held his hands tight to his sides and stood at attention beside his seat. Mrs. Harvey began to explain the alphabet.

A stood for Adam. "In Adam's fall, we sinned all," he had to say.

There was no music in the alphabet, no fun in standing so still. Stephen could not bear it.

His eyes filled with tears; his hands clenched. He gave a whoop and a yell and turned and ran out of the door. He kept on yelling and running down the road until he reached home. He ran past the house, down the hill, past Foster's Spring and into a stretch of woods where there was a brook that he liked.

Panting and out of breath, he fell on his stomach beside the brook, and buried his face in his arms. No more alphabet! No more school!

He lay there until he felt calm.

He began to listen to his favorite sounds. He could hear the water in the shallow brook gurgling over the stones. He could hear the birds in the trees overhead. When a breeze blew, even the trees made soft sounds.

Stephen rolled over on his back and looked up into the branches. "Everything sings!" he whispered. "Everything sings!"

THE FIRST FLUTE

CHAPTER

3

IT TOOK SOME COAXING to get Stephen back to school. With Morrison holding one hand and Dunning the other, the three brothers walked down the road.

"Don't worry about school, Stephie," said one.

"We'll take care of you, Stephie," promised the other.

Mrs. Foster had a talk with Mrs. Harvey.

"You see, Mrs. Harvey. Stephie has been sick so much I guess we've spoiled him. He's the baby of the family, too."

Mrs. Harvey understood. She had had a lot of experience with children. She realized that it would be easy to spoil such an attractive boy. Stephen Foster had a sensitive face and large, brown eyes.

Stephen recovered from his first fright, and promised to go to school. He usually did, although once in a while he wandered off to listen to the sing-ing birds. The teacher made allowances for him. She found that he was bright, often a lot brighter than the other children.

School for the very young finished early, and in May Stephen was free. He could lie on his stomach by the brook. He could stand by the road and listen to the drivers of covered wagons bellowing to the oxen: "Oh-ho-haw!"

"Take me down to hear the steamboat whistle?" he begged his mother.

"Be patient," said Mrs. Foster.

He ran after Henrietta.

But everybody was too busy, because the Fosters were moving to another house.

Father had a new job.

"I am going to be the first Collector of Tolls on the new Pittsburgh Canal," he told his family proudly when he came home one evening. "So we have to move across the Allegheny River to Alle-gheny Town. That's where the toll station is."

Mrs. Foster threw up her hands when she heard that.

"What a dreamer you are," she said to Mr. Foster. "Always dreaming and drifting from one job to another. You have so much ability, but you don't stay on one job long enough to show how clever you are. Stephie takes after you."

Father was always doing something different. Sometimes he was in politics, and then for a while he bought and sold houses. When he heard that the state of Pennsylvania was building a new canal, he decided that a job on the canal would be more interesting.

He picked Stephie up and hugged him. So Stephie took after him, did he? Well, he and Stephie both knew that dreaming was fun.

"Will there be woods and a brook where we are going?" asked Stephen.

"Of course!" his father promised.

"Will there be steamboats where we are going?" Stephen wanted to know.

"Yes," said his mother. "We are just moving across the river."

As soon as they had moved, Stephen went exploring and found plenty of woods and fields around their new house. He could still run down to the docks and watch the steamboats ply up and down the river, or make friends with the Negroes. They sang and danced and played their banjos on this side of the river the way they did in Pittsburgh. Sometimes they sang of things that Stephen had never seen: sugar cane and plantations and cotton picking. They shuffled and danced and held Stephen's hand while he learned their dances, or they took him in their laps and taught him their songs.

The Fosters went back to Pittsburgh often to the stores and to visit with their old friends.

"Let's go shopping, Stephen," said Mrs. Foster one day as she put on her black net gloves.

She and Stephen drove across the bridge in a horse and carriage.

"Will we visit Dunning?" asked Stephen.

"No, dear. Dunning has to work. He can't have visitors."

Twelve-year-old Dunning had a job in a book store in Pittsburgh.

When Stephen and his mother reached Pittsburgh, they went into a music store, because somebody in the family always needed sheet music.

Seven-year-old Stephen stared in wonder at all the musical instruments in the store: violins, harps, pianos, trumpets, flutes. Every one of them could make beautiful tones. When he saw a toy flute on the counter, the temptation was too much for him. He reached up on tiptoe and took it down. Blowing gently into the mouthpiece on the end and holding his fingertips over the holes in the side, he started to play. In a few minutes everyone in the store stopped and stared at the small boy, because he was playing "Hail Columbia!" And he was playing it perfectly!

"Who is that child?"

"That's one of the Foster boys."

Stephen played another tune, while his mother stood by and admired him.

"Has your son had many lessons, Mrs. Foster?" asked the shopkeeper.

"He hasn't had any lessons at all," she answered. "He's very talented, I guess."

The Fosters didn't have much money at that time, but Stephen's mother knew how happy the toy flute would make him. So she bought it for him.

After that they heard no more drum around the house. Instead, the flute shrilled tune after tune in their ears.

Stephen was learning to play the piano, too. First Henrietta sat with him at the keyboard and showed him how to read notes, and at last Mrs. Foster decided that he must have piano lessons. When the music teacher came to the house to give Stephen's sisters their lessons, Mrs. Foster told him to teach Stephen, too.

All the rest of the summer Stephen reveled in his music, as he learned about measures and beating out time and scales. Measures were little cages or compartments to capture melodies. Beating out time was like the strumming of a banjo or trotting horses' feet. And scales were the alphabet, only the alphabet was interesting when it ran up and down the piano. And when the order of the alphabet was changed, all sorts of tunes came out. C-E-G-C was a melody. C-C-D-E was "Yankee Doodle."

When he discovered a melody on the piano, Stephie would try it on his flute. "I can find the notes on my flute, too!" he would say. "Listen to me! Listen to me!"

In the autumn school had to be faced. Stephen and Morrison went to the Allegheny Academy where the Reverend Joseph Stockton was the principal. Reverend Stockton was strict but kindly, and Stephen liked him.

With this new teacher Stephen learned to accept school, and he never again ran out of the classroom yelling. Sometimes his writing ran up and down hill, but he was a good student.

"How is Stephen making out?"

"I guess he likes school," Morrison would say.

His family stopped worrying about him for a while.

"Maybe Stephen will become interested in something besides music," they sighed.

MINSTREL SHOWS

CHAPTER
4

MUSIC WAS ALL STE-
phen cared about, no
matter how hard he tried. While he learned Latin
verbs or struggled with arithmetic, songs danced
through his head. If the classroom window was open
on a warm day, he could hear the darkies singing
and strumming their banjos.

"Would you like to see a real minstrel show?"
his father asked him one day.

Nine-year-old Stephen had never seen a minstrel
show.

"In a minstrel show," Mr. Foster explained,
"actors blacken their faces with burnt cork and
imitate Negroes."

"They dress like darkies and play banjos," put in
Morrison.

"They dance jigs and tell jokes," added Dunning.

"Can we go soon?" begged Stephen.

"This Saturday night," Mr. Foster promised.

So on Saturday the Fosters got into their carriage and drove to Pittsburgh to the theater.

"Minstrel shows are popular everywhere these days," Mr. Foster said as the carriage wheels rumbled over the bridge. "They started when an actor named Thomas Rice, called 'Daddy Rice,' was trying to think of a new idea for an act. Strolling through the streets of a Kentucky town, Daddy Rice saw an old slave singing and dancing. The old darkie was amusing himself. He sang:

'First on de heel tap, den on de toe,
    Ebery time I wheel about I jump Jim Crow.' "

The Foster boys clapped their hands in unison as their father finished the jingle:

" 'Wheel about and turn about and do jis so,
    And every time I wheel about I jump Jim Crow.'

"Well," Mr. Foster went on, "Daddy Rice rushed up to the slave, borrowed his ragged coat and old straw hat. That night he blackened his face and went out on the stage and imitated the old slave. He danced the jig and sang 'Jim Crow.' The audience applauded and applauded. Daddy Rice traveled from city to city acting 'Jim Crow.' Other actors copied the idea. Soon there were whole groups of actors, called minstrel shows, who blackened their faces and sang Negro songs and danced Negro dances."

Stephen was so excited he could hardly sit still.

"Be careful, Stephie," said his mother. "Don't fall out of the carriage."

Soon they were in their seats in the theater and the curtains parted to show the whole company of actors. Stephen watched the dances; he swayed back and forth to the songs. "Coal Black Rose," the minstrels sang, and "Jump Jim Crow." When the curtains closed and the show was over, he begged his father to bring him again.

When the Fosters returned to their house in Allegheny, Stephen surprised them by singing the songs from memory. He even jumped up and danced the jigs. He picked up his flute—by this time he owned a real flute that his father had given him—and played "Coal Black Rose."

"Let's give a show of our own," he said to his brothers.

And so Morrison, Dunning, and Stephen gathered together all the boys of the neighborhood and called themselves a Thespian Society. They fixed a stage and set up benches in an old carriage house and invited all the adults to come and see their minstrel show.

Stephen Foster was the star. After the other boys

—faces blackened—had sung their songs and told their jokes, Stephen came out on the stage. He was dressed in ragged clothes. He shuffled along and danced and sang "Jump Jim Crow."

The audience cheered and applauded. They called him back and made him do the number again. Stephen was by far the best actor of them all.

The boys gave three shows a week all summer and charged admission, and they earned enough to

Margaret Ayer.

go over to the Pittsburgh theater on Saturday nights to see real actors in real shows.

Without their own show the Foster boys would not have had any spending money at all, because Mr. Foster was not earning much. He had given up his job as Toll Taker on the canal and had opened a store in Pittsburgh. Each evening, when Mr. Foster came home, he said his store wasn't doing any business.

"Our country is in a terrible state of depression," he told Mrs. Foster.

Mrs. Foster agreed with him. There wasn't enough money around. Many people had no jobs at all.

"I wish I could have more music lessons," Stephen dreamed out loud one day, and when Mr. Foster heard that he said sadly, "We just can't afford it right now, Stephie."

Stephen's sisters helped him with his music, but Eliza and Henrietta were both married and living in houses of their own. They lived in the same town of Allegheny and they visited home often, but not often enough for Stephen.

He read what books he could find around the house about the great composers—Mozart and Beethoven. There were not many, because the rest of the Fosters liked music just for fun. They shook their heads when they saw the youngest member of the family practicing the piano so long. Or spelling his way through books that were too old for him. Or drawing lines on paper and trying to write down his own melodies.

"Put aside that music and do your lessons, Stephie dear," his mother would say.

By that time Stephie was eleven. He was growing so gentle and shy and quiet that his family always spoke to him in a kindly way.

Stephen and Morrison were doing their schoolwork with a tutor, the Reverend Nathan Todd, who taught the boys Latin and Greek and English. He, too, noticed how well behaved Stephen was.

"Stephen is the most perfect gentleman I ever had for a pupil," Mr. Todd told Mr. Foster.

Stephen knew that school was easier and over with sooner if he behaved himself and studied. He preferred to wait patiently until school was out, then wander off to a quiet place and play his flute.

One day in the early spring he came home from school and didn't feel like playing his flute. He didn't feel like doing anything. He wasn't hungry. He began to cough.

"Oh, dear!" said Mrs. Foster. "That sounds like whooping cough."

"Is Stephie sick again?"

The whole household was upset. The family doctor came, and when he examined Stephen he nodded his head.

"He has whooping cough again. Give him some tartar and cochineal and sugar dissolved in warm water."

Stephen made a face. Every time he started to cough the doctor gave him tartar and cochineal. But Mother had a way of putting an arm around her youngest while she held the spoon. Down went the terrible dose.

The cough lasted until the end of June. So there was no more school that year for Stephen, and not much music either.

STEPHEN WRITES A WALTZ

CHAPTER
5

STEPHEN'S MOTHER and father felt more and more disappointed in Stephen as time went on. The other Foster boys were successful. Henry was working for a company in Pittsburgh; Dunning was with a steamboat company, keeping books and making out bills. A letter had come from William telling the family that he had obtained a position as principal engineer of canals and railroads of eastern Pennsylvania. He was moving to a fine new house in Towanda.

Everyone was talking about railroads in those days, because they were something new. There was even talk of building a railroad as far as Pittsburgh.

"Are you interested in railroads, Stephen?" asked his father.

The boy shook his head.

Mrs. Foster had another idea.

"Now that the depression is about over and your father has a new job with the government, I think we can give you more music lessons," she said.

Stephen hugged his mother when he heard that. She always understood him. Even though she was as disappointed as her husband, Mrs. Foster arranged to have Mr. Henry Kleber, who owned a music store in Pittsburgh, come to the house and give Stephen lessons.

When Mr. Foster saw Stephen spending so much time at the piano he said, "I'm going to write to William about Stephen. Perhaps he can suggest something."

Stephen didn't know William very well, because William had left home the year Stephen was born, and only came back for short visits once in a great while, but Henrietta or Ann Eliza often said, "William is like a second father in the family."

Sometimes Mrs. Foster sighed and said, "William has been so good to us! During the depression he even sent us money so that we could get along."

Stephen wondered what William would suggest for him. He didn't want to build railroads. He didn't want to work for a steamboat company. He didn't want to be a bookkeeper. He just wanted to learn more about music.

But before his father could write to William,

another letter arrived saying that William was coming home for a visit.

That was joyous news! Mrs. Foster hurried to tell her married daughters and they came back to the house with their husbands and children to help prepare for William. They fixed all kinds of food: pumpkin pies, apples, cider, roast meat, turkey, almonds, raisins, squash, Indian corn bread, wild plum jam.

Henry ran errands and brought packages home from the stores. Dunning, Morrison, and Stephen had to carry a lot of coal for all the cooking in the kitchen stove and for the fireplace in the parlor.

They listened for sleigh bells, for it was winter, and the ground was covered with hard, white snow.

At last they heard him, and everybody ran to the door. There was William! He was so successful that he drove up in his own sleigh with two horses.

"Hello, Mother and Father," called William. "Hello, everybody!"

Everyone talked at once and crowded around William while he took off his coat and muffler and hat.

"Have Morrison and Stephen been good boys?" he asked.

"We're not boys any more," said Morrison. "I'm sixteen."

"I'm thirteen!" chimed in Stephen.

After dinner William wanted to know all the family news.

"Why isn't Henry married?" asked William.

"He can't make up his mind which girl he likes best!" laughed Morrison.

"What are you going to do, Morrison?"

"Morrison has just started on his first job," said Mrs. Foster proudly. "He's working at the cotton factory in Pittsburgh, keeping records and carrying messages around town."

"What about you, Stephen?" William asked.

What, indeed! What could Stephen do? He wasn't strong enough for heavy work.

The family circle sat silent for a moment, looking at its youngest member.

"I have an idea," said William. "Why not let Stephen come back to Towanda with me? There's a good school nearby where he can go. I think he's just spoiled from being with his family so much."

Stephen looked at his oldest brother. William seemed handsome and interesting, but not familiar. He seemed kind and understanding, too; so perhaps it would be fun to visit with him—for a while.

"Do I have to stay away from you forever?" he asked his mother.

The whole family laughed at that. Stephen was such a baby, even though he was thirteen!

"Just for a few months, Stephen," his father

said. "While you go to school. I think William is right. Your family spoils you too much."

In a few days William's visit came to an end, and he and Stephen climbed into the big sleigh. Stephen was wearing a warm coat buttoned up tight and a cap pulled down over his ears. Mother tied a woolen scarf around his head, too, so that he wouldn't get a sore throat from the cold air. She hugged him as though she didn't want him to leave. William tucked the fur robe around him.

"Remember that he's not very strong!" said Mrs. Foster.

The air was cold. The horses pawed the ground to be off. William gave the reins a tug. and the bells jingled as the sleigh sped over the hard snow.

Stephen looked back at his family standing on the porch and his mother holding a handkerchief to her eyes.

"Good-by! Good-by!" the Fosters called after them.

"Will we be there tonight?" asked Stephen.

"Oh, no!" William told him.

The journey was long. They traveled all morning, stopping at an inn for dinner. They whisked through the cold air all afternoon, and at night they stopped at another inn. After almost a week they reached Towanda.

"Are we still in Pennsylvania?" asked Stephen.

"Yes, indeed! Pennsylvania is a big state. You would have to travel still longer to reach Philadelphia. Some day there will be a railroad to Pittsburgh so that you will be able to travel much faster than a horse and sleigh."

Stephen found that he couldn't stay with Brother William all of the time, but only when school was closed. The rest of the time he lived at Athens Academy in Tioga Point near Towanda.

Athens Academy was very different from going to lessons with Reverend Stockton, who had taught only a handful of boys. There were two hundred students at Tioga Point. The school building was two stories tall, made of wood and painted white.

Young Stephen, away from home for the first time in his life, didn't have his mother and sisters hovering over him. He was living with husky boys who ran hard and played rough games. If he couldn't keep up, his schoolmates rushed off and left him.

He grew more lonesome every day; he became nervous and couldn't sleep at night.

"Please let me come and live with you in Towanda," he wrote to William.

William wrote back and asked Stephen to stay at Tioga Point a little longer. Perhaps he would get used to the place.

So the sorrowful Stephen went to classes to study

grammar, arithmetic, history, and bookkeeping. He was able to take a course in music, and he liked art, too. He liked painting pictures with water colors, and he even wrote poetry for his English class.

Gradually he got acquainted with the other boys, and they began to like him. When they found that he could play the flute so well, they realized that he must be rather special. Stephen played a clarinet in the school band and made friends with the other band members.

But he was still a boy who did not always come to class, a boy who liked to wander off listening for new melodies in the streams and woods. As soon as the snow had melted off the ground the wanderlust overcame him. Once in a while he could persuade a classmate to play truant with him, and instead of going to school the boys would stroll into the meadow picking strawberries or wading barefoot in brooks. They frequently wandered far enough so that they could not hear the school bell.

On moonlight nights the students went on boating parties on the Susquehanna River, right by Tioga Point, and they always invited Steve.

"Come boating with us, Steve."

Stephen liked that. He liked to lie back in a boat and look up at the stars, while the boats floated along on the glistening water, and the students sang as he played his flute.

Still he was homesick. He wanted to be with his family, with his mother and father and sisters, with Morrison and Dunning, with the Negroes that he knew.

As he sat in his room one day trying to study, he looked out of the window, at the woods and fields around the school. In the distance the Susquehanna River sparkled in the sun. Ti-o-ga, Ti-o-ga, he thought dreamily, and a new melody began to run through his mind. Suddenly excited, Stephen pushed aside his books and snatched a piece of paper to write the melody down before he could forget it. He worked all afternoon on the piece. When it was finished, he rushed off with it to his music teacher.

The teacher was surprised and pleased.

"What have you called it?" he asked.

" 'The Tioga Waltz,' " said Stephen.

Stephen became famous all over the school when the other students learned about "The Tioga Waltz."

"Do you mean you've written some music, Steve?" they would ask.

"Play it for us, Steve."

"It is to be played by three flutes and a piano," Stephen explained.

Soon Stephen and three others were practicing the new number, and in April, when the school gave its exhibition, Stephen played his composition before a large audience.

"Who is that attractive young man?" the visitors wanted to know.

"That's Stephen Foster."

The attractive young man was fifteen. He stood very straight when he played his flute. Even though he was too thin, he was handsome, with brown eyes and black hair that he brushed down hard. His face was unusually serious as he held his flute to his lips to play his "Tioga Waltz."

"OH! SUSANNA"

CHAPTER

6

AFTER STEPHEN HAD been at Athens Academy a year and a half, he begged to go home. He wrote to William again and again. At last William gave in and wrote to the Fosters in Allegheny and explained,

"Stephen is very unhappy at Athens Academy. I think I shall send him home."

So Stephen was allowed to leave Tioga Point. His father next sent him to Jefferson College in Canonsburg, Pennsylvania. It was no use. Stephen was homesick. In seven days he came back to Allegheny, and his family didn't try to send him away to school again.

The household had changed somewhat while he was at Tioga Point and Canonsburg. His sister Henrietta with her husband and three small children had moved back into the Foster house in Allegheny, and Stephen liked that. Henrietta was only seven years older than he, and now that he was grown she seemed closer to his own age. She made the happy family circle happier. But Dunning had left home.

As soon as he returned from Towanda, Stephen had asked, "Where is Dunning?"

And his mother had explained that Dunning was now working for a steamship company in Cincinnati.

"Dunning is twenty; he's a grown man, now, Stephie dear," his mother said.

Stephen still had Morrison, only three years older, and always his best companion. And he still had the Negroes. Now that he was home he could wander down to the docks and listen to their songs and watch their dancing.

Stephen Foster just settled down into his protective family and the childhood scenes that he loved so much and forgot the rest of the world. He wrote little songs to entertain his companions; he dreamed away the days and months.

With Stephen home in the evenings, the Fosters had musical evenings again when the neighbors dropped in.

"Let's have a singing club," someone suggested.

It was agreed. The Fosters and their friends formed a singing club, that met around the Foster piano twice a week. Stephen was writing music all the time, now, and he always had a new Negro song or a special piece for them.

"What's our surprise this week, Stephen?" they asked one night.

Stephen waved a piece of music paper in the air and said,

"Here it is. A whole new song."

"Sing it for us! Sing it for us!"

Stephen sat down at the piano and began:

"Oh! Belle, don't you tell,
Don't tell Massa,
Don't you, Belle.
Oh! Belle, de Lou'siana Belle,
I's gwine to marry you,
Lou'siana Belle."

His friends crowded around him excited and sang "Lou'siana Belle" again and again and again. Soon everybody in town was singing "Lou'siana Belle."

A few months later Stephen's singing club was overjoyed when he wrote them still another song: "Uncle Ned."

"There was an old darkie,
They called him Uncle Ned,
He's dead long ago, long ago—"

That was all very well. But by this time Stephen was twenty years old. He was a grown man who ought to be earning a living.

"You will have to do something, Stephen," said his father. "You can't just sit home writing pretty tunes."

So it was decided that Stephen should go to Cincinnati and work in the same office with his brother Dunning. Leaving home meant leaving the family, the singing club, his mother and sisters and brother Morrison. It meant that he would have to pay attention to unpleasant tasks as he had at school. But at least he could see Dunning once more.

He boarded one of the riverboats and traveled downstream to Cincinnati. There he sat on a high stool working as a bookkeeper alongside of his brother, making entries in huge books. His desk was right in front of a window that looked out over the Ohio River, and on the other side of the river was Kentucky.

"Pay attention to your work, Steve," Dunning cautioned him. "You mustn't dream here, or you'll make a mistake, and the books won't balance."

Stephen worked hard most of the time. He paid close attention to the numbers that he wrote in columns. But there right outside of his window was the dock where the steamboats came in. A Negro was sitting on the dock strumming a banjo. The

sun was so hot that nobody was moving around.
Suddenly Stephen heard a whistle in the distance.
The Negro put down his banjo and jumped up.

"Steamboat's comin'!" he shouted.

Stephen could work no more. He dropped his pen and ran out to the dock with everyone else to watch the white boat come puffing up the river, the big wheel churning up the water at its side. The boat was coming from the Southland, bringing travelers from Louisiana, Mississippi, Tennessee, and Alabama.

When Stephen was excited his heart and head

filled with songs, old tunes and new, and before he knew it he was singing.

"Oh, I come from Alabama—"

Why, that was a new melody! He took out his pad and pencil and sat down on the dock, thinking of the new melody and the strum, strum, strum of the banjo he had just heard the Negro playing.

The boat was still chugging up the river, turning its bow into the dock, its decks crowded with passengers.

"Oh, I come from Alabama with my banjo on my knee—"

While crowds bustled back and forth in front of him, Stephen wrote on until he had finished the whole song.

"I come from Alabama with my
    banjo on my knee;
I's gwine to Lou'siana,
My true love for to see.
It rained all night the day I left,
The weather it was dry;
The sun so hot I froze to death,
Susanna, don't you cry.

Oh! Susanna, do not cry for me.
I come from Alabama with my
    banjo on my knee."

Stephen Foster took the song to Mr. William C. Peters. Mr. Peters, who was in the music business in Cincinnati, had once lived in Pittsburgh and had come to the Foster house to give music lessons to the Foster girls. He was the only one in Cincinnati whom Stephen knew who might want to publish a song. Mr. Peters liked "Oh! Susanna."

"Yes," he said to Stephen. "I think this song will be successful."

"Thank you, Mr. Peters," said Stephen, and he never asked for any money.

Mr. Peters printed copies of "Oh! Susanna" and immediately began selling it everywhere. People loved the song. They played it on their pianos, guitars, and banjos. Minstrel shows sang it.

Adventurers traveling to California to look for gold sang it. When the news got around that gold had been discovered in the Sacramento Valley, hundreds of men and women put all their furniture and clothes into covered wagons and started West. Because it was in the year 1849 they were called "Forty-niners." As their wagons rolled along over the desert and across the Rocky Mountains, the Forty-niners sang "Oh! Susanna."

When the wagon trains stopped at night, the Forty-niners sat around their camp fires singing, "Oh! Susanna, do not cry for me. I come from Alabama with my banjo on my knee."

STEPHEN IS FAMOUS

CHAPTER
7

MR. PETERS PAID
Stephen Foster only a
hundred dollars for "Oh! Susanna." He sold thousands of copies and made thousands of dollars for
himself.

Stephen didn't have much business sense. He
didn't realize how important "Oh! Susanna" was.
He thought a hundred dollars was a great deal of
money.

"Have you written any other songs?" asked Mr.
Peters.

"Yes," said Stephen Foster. "I have two, called
'Lou'siana Belle' and 'Uncle Ned.' Would you like
to see them?"

"Yes, indeed!"

"Lou'siana Belle" and "Uncle Ned" were already
popular around Pittsburgh and Cincinnati. When
Mr. Peters printed them and sold copies, they be-

came popular everywhere: in Philadelphia, in Louisiana, in New York, even in London. Minstrel shows especially liked Stephen Foster's songs, because they were about the Negroes.

Stephen's songs were on display in the stores. If Mrs. Foster went shopping in Pittsburgh, she could go into the music store and see her own son's music for sale.

"Do you remember the seven-year-old boy who once played the toy flute so well?" she asked the storekeeper.

The storekeeper remembered.

"He's twenty-one years old now," Mrs. Foster said proudly. "He wrote 'Oh! Susanna.'"

When the Foster family went to Pittsburgh on Saturday night to see a minstrel show, actors with blackened faces were singing "Uncle Ned" and "Lou'siana Belle" and "Oh! Susanna," Stephen's songs!

Stephen sat on his high stool in the steamship company office and tried to pay attention to his work. It was no use. Bookkeeping grew duller and duller. Dunning had grown tired of it, too, by that time, because one day he said,

"Steve, I've joined the army. I'm going to Texas and fight in the war against Mexico."

Stephen stayed on alone in the steamship office for a few months after his brother had left, until he could stand the columns of figures no longer.

"No more bookkeeping for me," he decided one day. "I'm going to earn my living writing songs."

He left his job in Cincinnati and went home to Allegheny to live with his family. His mother and father were happy to have him back with them.

"It's good to have you home, Stephen," they all said.

"It's good to be home," said Stephen.

At last his family understood how important music was to Stephen. At last they were willing to let him spend his time writing pretty tunes. They gave him a room in the back of the house on the second floor where he could work and study. There he had his piano, and there he settled down to write songs, songs, songs.

Stephen felt truly happy for the first time in his life. He could stay indoors and work as long as he felt like it. He could take long walks in the woods and listen to the birds, the rustling leaves, the brooks. He could go down to the docks and talk to the Negroes and listen to their songs. He could watch the steamboats come and go. He could sit under a shade tree and play his flute.

Morrison was still around, and Henry was married and he and his wife were living with the Fosters. That made the family circle even bigger. At last even Dunning came back from the Mexican war. He was tired and sick from so many battles, and he wanted to be home where he could be looked after.

"I hear you're famous," Dunning said to Stephen. "They were even singing 'Oh! Susanna' down in Texas."

The Fosters all nodded. They were proud of Stephen now.

Stephen was the same, though; always getting sick. He was home just a short time when he came down with a fever. The doctor thought it was malaria. It was summertime, and hot, and Stephen lay in bed feeling hotter. His mother hovered over him, putting cold cloths on his head. He was still her youngest.

Stephen felt weak and shaky for a long time afterward. But he was home where he could rest. No more hurrying to an office. No more working on books all day long.

He didn't realize how famous he really was, until he received a letter from New York.

"Will you please allow us to publish some of your songs?" asked the important music company, Firth, Pond & Co. "We will pay you two cents on every copy we sell."

Two cents on every copy! That was many times better than a hundred dollars a song. "Oh! Susanna" had sold thousands and thousands of copies.

Stephen became excited. So did the whole Foster family. Maybe he could earn a good living writing songs after all. Stephen wrote to Firth, Pond & Co. and accepted the offer.

Soon another letter came from a company in Baltimore, F. D. Benteen, who also wanted to publish some of his songs. Stephen Foster accepted their offer, too.

Then he really settled down to work, his head a whirlwind of ideas, tunes, jumbles of rhyming words. The piano in his workroom tinkled and jingled, and his light showed under his door late into the night, as he wrote one song after another. He turned out fourteen songs in a year, his excitement burning on and on. Firth, Pond & Co. received "Nelly Was a Lady," "My Brudder Gum," and "Nelly Bly." Benteen received "Oh! Lemuel" and "Dolly Day."

Some of these songs were successful; some were not. The one that really set the whole world a-singing was one that he sent to Benteen, called "Camptown Races."

Fragments of its trotting rhythm had probably been dancing through his imagination since boyhood. Since the days when he had stood at the road and watched travelers trot by on horseback, or rode in the family carriage behind the horse that clip-clopped, clip-clopped along.

"The Camptown ladies sing this song,
Doo-dah! doo-dah!
The Camptown race track five miles long,
Oh! doo-dah-day!
I come down there with my hat caved in,
Doo-dah! doo-dah!
I go back home with a pocket full of tin,
Oh! doo-dah-day!
Gwine to run all night!
Gwine to run all day!
I'll bet my money on the bob-tail nag,
Somebody bet on the bay."

Everybody who heard the song fell in love with the tune and the rhythm and the words that had no meaning: Doo-dah! Doo-dah! People loved to whistle the tune and sing, Doo-dah! Doo-dah!, finishing up with, "Oh! doo-dah-day!"

STEPHEN FALLS IN LOVE

CHAPTER

8

TEPHEN WAS HAND-some as well as famous. More neighbors than ever dropped in at the Foster house in the evening, often bringing their daughters, because their daughters insisted upon coming. The young ladies wanted to meet this handsome and interesting man who wrote such beautiful songs.

They noted, though, that Stephen favored Susan Pentland who sang soprano in the "Stephen Foster Quartet."

As Stephen directed his quartet and listened to Susan's high, sweet voice, he thought he must be falling in love with her. Perhaps he ought to be writing a love song, or two, instead of "Oh! doo-dah-day!"

One evening another young lady joined the quartet. She was Jane McDowell, the daughter of an important doctor in Pittsburgh. Stephen was watching Susan when Jane started to sing, and the lovely contralto voice made him forget Susan completely. He began to watch Jane. Jane had curly light brown hair and blue eyes. She wore a pale pink summer dress with delicate ruffles around the neck. He felt sure he had never seen anyone so beautiful.

After Jane had come to a few practices, Stephen decided definitely that he was falling in love with her. He waited all one evening for a chance to speak to her. At last he got up his courage and said, "May I come to see you at your home?"

After that Stephen was not always home in the evening for singing, unless Jane was there, too. When friends dropped in and found Stephen out, they knew he was visiting with Jane McDowell. When they found him in and no Jane, they knew another young man was calling on Jane.

Jane was being courted by a young lawyer, and Stephen knew it.

"I'm not as tall and strong as he," Stephen thought. "Jane will probably marry him. His family is wealthy, and mine is not."

"I think she prefers you, Stephen," Morrison said. "I really think she prefers you."

Stephen was not so sure. He tried to look his best whenever he was with her. On his evening to call he would have his hair slicked back hard and he would be wearing a stiff white collar. In his hand there was always a bouquet of flowers.

By some mistake one evening both men called at the McDowell house at the same time. Stephen arrived first. No sooner did he give Jane her flowers and sit down than the handsome young lawyer arrived with *his* bouquet of flowers.

Stephen was usually a sweet and gentle person. This time he was angry. He turned his chair so that his back was to Jane and the other suitor. He sat that way all evening and read a book. The lawyer knew that Stephen had arrived first. He stayed anyway, talking to Jane until after ten o'clock. At last he got up to go.

He bowed to Stephen's back and said, "Good evening, sir."

Stephen wouldn't speak to him; he wouldn't even turn around.

As soon as the visitor had left, Stephen jumped up and took hold of Jane's hands.

"Now, Miss Jane," he said. "I want your answer! Is it yes, or is it no?"

Jane said *yes* to Stephen, and they were married July 22, 1850. After a big family wedding, they traveled to Baltimore and New York on their honeymoon.

They came back in September and moved into the Foster house in Allegheny, to join the family circle again, the only place where Stephen could be really happy. He was still the baby, still the favorite. He still needed more looking after than anyone else, even though he was now a married man.

As soon as he and Jane were settled, he went to his workroom in the back of the house and began to write. He worked harder than his family had ever seen him work before, trying out new tunes on the piano or working with pen and paper until late at night. In his first year of married life he wrote more than a dozen songs.

If he had difficulty with a melody or finding exactly the right words for a new song, he would often ask a member of the family to help him with it. Jane gave him what help she could; she sang for him or listened carefully while he played a new number. But oftener than not it was his brother Morrison, closest to Stephen in age, to whom he turned.

Morrison, now twenty-seven, was working in the office of a cotton mill in Pittsburgh. He was not at all surprised when one day Stephen walked into his office, sat down, and said:

"I have a new song, but the words don't seem quite right."

The song began,

"Way down upon the Pedee River—"

"What's a good name of two syllables for a Southern river?" Stephen asked. "I don't like Pe-dee."

"How about Yazoo?" asked Morrison.

"No, that's been used before."

Morrison took down an atlas from the top of his desk, and the two men looked at it together. In Florida they found a tiny river that neither had ever heard of before: the Swanee River.

"That's fine!" said Stephen, and he dashed away to finish his song.

In a few days he showed the results to his family.

"Way down upon the Swanee River,
Far, far away,
There's where my heart is turning ever,
There's where the old folks stay.
All up and down the whole creation,
Sadly I roam,
Still longing for the old plantation,
And for the old folks at home.
All the world is sad and dreary,
Every where I roam,
Oh! darkies how my heart grows weary,
Far from the old folks at home."

"Old Folks at Home," was soon being sung all over the world. No song has ever been loved by more people.

"JEANIE WITH THE LIGHT BROWN HAIR"

CHAPTER

9

THE NEXT YEAR Stephen Foster's daughter, Marian, was born. A child of his own made him feel still more ambitious to write songs and earn money. A new baby meant more expenses: doctor's bills, a nurse—

At the same time it meant a lot of excitement around the house. Everybody in town came in to see the new baby. The baby cried. The members of the household rushed around doing things.

"I can't get any work done here," Stephen realized.

He found himself a small office in town. Every day, instead of going to his room at the back of the house, he went to his office.

"I'm glad you have an office," said his wife, Jane. "You seem more like a businessman."

Jane Foster never quite understood why a man

should stay home to work. She had never known any song writers before.

Stephen sat at his desk in his new office and tried to think of different ways to make money with his songs. His songs were most popular with minstrel companies. The minstrels! Of course! He would try them.

He wrote to one of the most important men in the minstrel show business, Mr. E. P. Christy. Everybody knew about Christy's minstrels. They gave shows in the most important theaters all over the country—in Buffalo, New York City, Philadelphia, Pittsburgh.

"I have just written a new song," Stephen's letter said to Mr. Christy. "It will be published soon. How would you like to have the song first? Then Christy's minstrels can sing it for a while before it is published. You can pay me ten dollars for the privilege of introducing my new song."

Mr. Christy knew Stephen Foster's songs perfectly well. He knew how suitable they were for minstrel shows, and he wrote back right away:

"Enclosed is ten dollars. Please send me the song."

The song that Mr. Christy received from Stephen Foster was "Oh! Boys, Carry Me Along." Parts of the melody were from tunes that he had heard the Negroes sing in Lieve's church when he was a small boy. His own daughter had reminded him of the nurse he had had when he was small. Lieve had taken him to church with her, and there he had heard wonderful music. He could remember many of the Negro melodies. He loved them so much that his songs were often like them. He had put some of them into "Oh! Boys, Carry Me Along."

"Oh! boys, carry me 'long;
Carry me till I die—
Carry me down to the burying ground,
Massa, don't you cry."

"Please remember that this is a sad song," Stephen cautioned Mr. Christy.

Stephen sent Christy other songs, too. One of them was "Massa's in the Cold, Cold Ground."

Stephen knew that Negro songs were best for minstrels, so that was the kind he wrote.

When his publishers heard about it, they disapproved. They thought he ought to write songs about white folk. Stephen pondered. He needed money for his wife and baby. When Christy's Minstrels introduced one of his songs, it became popular at once, and sold a lot of copies.

On the other hand, maybe his publishers were right. Maybe he ought to try to build up his reputation as a composer of white songs, too. But Stephen needed money.

"Leave my name off the Negro songs," Stephen

said to Christy. "Pretend that you wrote them, and put your name on."

They did so. Stephen's new Negro songs came out in the stores with Christy's name on them and not Stephen's.

The songs became popular so fast that Stephen grew unhappy about it. He wanted the public to know he had written them. He particularly wanted the public to know that he had written "Massa's in the Cold, Cold Ground."

"I have changed my mind," he wrote to Mr. Christy. "I have decided that I want my own name on all of my songs. I shall return your money, if you will put my name on instead of yours."

Stephen's brothers sided with him, too. As long as Negro songs were becoming so popular—especially Stephen's—they wanted Stephen to have the credit.

But Christy had made a bargain. He didn't give in for a long time, and several years passed before Stephen's songs—the ones he had sold to Christy—came out with his own name on them. In time everybody knew they were written by none other than the great Stephen Foster.

Great or not, Stephen still felt lonely at times, even though he had a wife and baby, even though he had his parents and brothers and sisters. He still liked to wander off into the woods or linger on the docks with the Negroes. He could never seem to stay at one thing very long, but drifted from his piano to the out-of-doors or to the waterfront.

"I guess I must be a restless person," he decided.

He loved his home and his family—loved everyone around him—but he couldn't feel content. Always within him there were more melodies to be captured and put upon paper. His feelings of depression and sorrow were probably songs that needed to be written.

"Are you interested in anything besides music?" his wife asked him.

"No," he told her.

"Maybe if you had a steady job you would be happier."

He knew he didn't want a steady job.

Jane was tired of living in with her husband's family; she wanted a house of her own, and she needed things for herself and the baby. Stephen never made as much money as they needed. Jane became angry with Stephen. They argued about it.

Jane Foster became so angry that she packed her bag, picked up the baby, and left Stephen. She went home to her parents' house in Pittsburgh.

Deserted by his wife and baby, Stephen felt completely lost. He didn't even want to be with his family or talk to them, so he sold the few pieces of furniture that he and Jane owned and went to New York.

He was able to travel all the way by train, because his brother William and other engineers had just finished building the Pennsylvania Railroad as far as Pittsburgh.

In New York he found himself a cheap room and tried to work. Perhaps if he wrote a very successful song, it would earn a lot of money, and Jane would come back to him.

When he grew tired of working, he walked through the streets of New York trying to enjoy the sights. New York was a big city, more crowded than Pittsburgh, and noisier, too. It was hard to get acquainted and make friends in New York, and Stephen didn't know anybody except his publishers, Firth, Pond & Co. Stephen would walk until he began to hear in his mind an idea for a new song. Then he would go back to his room and try to write.

The songs he wrote while he was in New York were sad and showed plainly how homesick he felt. They were not very successful, either. He missed his family too much. He felt more depressed as each day passed. There was no gaiety in him to produce a song like "Oh! doo-dah-day!"

All he could think about was home, his old home. In summer the darkies were gay. His old home—

his old Kentucky home, sounded well. It began to sound like a song. His home wasn't in Kentucky, but that didn't matter. There was a beautiful old house in Bardstown, Kentucky, where he had once visited. The meadows that he loved—the meadows in bloom and full of flowers. And the birds that always made music. All these fragments and pieces of happy memories could make a song.

There it was on paper finally, after a lot of work:

"The sun shines bright
In my old Kentucky home.
'Tis summer the darkies are gay,
The corn top's ripe and the meadow's
    in the bloom,
While the birds make music all the day.
Weep no more, my lady.
Oh! weep no more today!
We will sing one song for the old
    Kentucky home,
For the old Kentucky home, far away."

The song was a success and earned some money, but the money was soon gone. Stephen was twenty-seven years old, and he still couldn't manage money. No matter how much he earned it never seemed to be as much as he needed.

At home either his mother or his wife saw to it that he had good meals, but in New York he didn't eat properly. He grew thinner. Not having enough to eat made him feel even more depressed and sad.

Jane Foster worried about Stephen, because she knew he didn't have sense enough to look after himself properly. At last she packed her bag once more, picked up the baby, and traveled all the way to New York. When she found Stephen, he and his room were both untidy. There were scraps of paper all over the floor, and the furniture was dusty. Stephen's clothes were wrinkled, his hair was mussed, and he was bothered by a nasty cough.

"Poor Stephen!" cried Jane. "I should never have left you."

Stephen was so happy to have Jane back with him that his depression and sorrow vanished, and he rushed out to find a house for them to live in. They moved to Bloomfield Street, Hoboken, New Jersey, just across the Hudson River from New York.

It wasn't long before he was back at the piano, running his fingers gaily up and down the keys, singing for Jane in the evening. He wrote his most beautiful love song for her while he felt so happy.

"I dream of Jeanie with the light brown hair,
  Borne, like a vapor, on the summer air;
  I see her tripping where the bright streams play,
  Happy as the daisies that dance on her way . . ."

His wife's nickname was really Jennie, and he called the song "Jennie with the Light Brown Hair." But somehow the publisher changed it to Jeanie, and that is what it has been ever since.

After they had been on Bloomfield Street a few months, Stephen's gaiety began to wear off and his feelings slumped. By this time Jane understood her husband, and she realized that he missed his family and the scenes of his boyhood. He could never be happy away from them.

"I'm really getting tired of Hoboken and New York," she said.

"So am I," Stephen agreed.

By the end of the year their minds were made up, and they packed their things and returned to Allegheny.

It was late at night when they reached the house. No sooner did Stephen walk up the front steps than he heard his mother inside say,

"Is that my dear son come back again?"

The whole family rushed out to welcome Jane and Stephen. Stephen was so glad to be home that he cried.

SORROW

CHAPTER
10

BESTED AND LOOKED after, Stephen should have felt happy again. But he didn't. He stayed thin. He grew tired easily.

"What's the matter with you, Stephen?" his family wanted to know.

Stephen couldn't tell them. He just knew that he didn't have any energy.

He didn't have much money, and he tried to write songs. He strove all the time for new melodies. In the evening he would sit at the piano, running his fingers over the keys, or playing songs he had already written. His eyes would fill with tears, if the song he was playing was sad.

If he thought of a new melody in the middle of the night, he would get up and light a candle and write the idea down before he could forget it.

Jane Foster was worried. She knew her husband's songs weren't as good as they used to be. He had attacks of chills and fever that kept him in bed for days at a time. His cough grew worse.

Stephen borrowed money from William and from Morrison and did his best to pay them back. Of course, they didn't care whether he repaid the loans, but he worried about it.

Stephen was still receiving money for his other songs; he had really been doing well for a while. He just seemed to spend more than he earned.

During the whole year 1855 he published only one or two songs. No matter how hard he worked, he couldn't seem to think of new melodies. The excitement he had felt when he wrote "Camptown Races" seemed to have died away completely. Maybe it was because 1855 was such a sorrowful year for Stephen Foster.

The first sorrow came when his mother got into her carriage and drove across the bridge to Pittsburgh to shop and chat with her lady friends. She went about her shopping first, and as she walked away from one of the stores where she had just bought some ribbon, Mrs. Foster felt faint and sank to the ground.

Passers-by rushed to help her, and since she was the mother of the famous Stephen Foster many of them recognized her. Word flew around that Stephen Foster's mother had taken ill in the street.

A small crowd gathered and with some difficulty she was carried to the home of a friend nearby. A doctor was called, but Mrs. Foster died before he arrived.

The suddenness of their mother's death was a terrible shock to the whole Foster family. For Stephen it was the hardest of all, because he had loved his mother so much. He simply sank down into a chair and wept.

Mourners and visitors filled the house for days and days, because Mrs. Foster had many friends.

A few months later Stephen's father died. Mr. Foster was old, and he had been sick a long time. When his wife died, the grief was too much for him. He just put his head back on the pillow, closed his eyes, and slipped quietly away.

Mourners and visitors filled the house again.

Stephen tried to settle down to work once more. The Foster home seemed big and empty with both his mother and his father gone.

He grew thinner and more nervous. He couldn't sleep at night. He was still sensitive to sounds. Pretty sounds—birds, rustling leaves, banjos— were a joy. Ugly sounds were another matter.

He had a clock in his bedroom that bothered him with its tick, tick, tick, tick. Until, one night when he could not get to sleep, he wrapped the clock in a blanket and hid it in a bureau drawer. He got back into bed, but he imagined he could still hear the clock. He got up again and took the clock all the way down to the cellar and hid it in a washtub. Then he climbed the two flights of stairs to his bedroom, sank wearily into bed and—at last—fell sound asleep.

Out in the world Stephen Foster was more famous than ever. His songs were popular everywhere. People whistled his tunes when they walked along the street or traveled by on horseback.

As the sorrow began to wear off the outside world began to hope for a new song from Stephen Foster. Would he ever feel happy enough to write another "Oh! doo-dah-day!"?

But Stephen was not through with sorrow. Or rather, sorrow was not through with Stephen.

Stephen had a lot of friends among children, because he and children usually liked the same things. One ten-year-old girl named Annie visited with Stephen often. They used to sit on the porch steps and chat, or stroll about together.

Annie's family sent her out on an errand on a rainy night. Covering her face with her shawl against the driving rain, without looking, she hurried across the street, right in front of a horse and carriage. The horse's feet trampled her to death.

When Stephen heard the terrible news he hurried to Annie's mother and father. He had so much sorrow in his own life that he could understand exactly how they felt about losing their little girl. He stayed with Annie's parents all night and did what he could to comfort them.

A few weeks later, when there were visitors in the parlor, Stephen came into the room. He had a piece of music in his hand.

"Oh, Stephen!" they all said. "Do you have a new song for us?"

"Yes," he replied.

His face was rather sad. So they waited until he was ready to sit down at the piano and play his new song. As soon as they heard the opening words, they understood. The song was "Gentle Annie."

"Thou wilt come no more, gentle Annie,
 Like a flow'r, thy spirit did depart,
 Thou art gone, alas! like the many
 That have bloomed in the summer of my heart."

"OLD BLACK JOE"

CHAPTER

11

THE FOSTER FAMILY was becoming scattered, so many of them had moved away by this time. Henry, Dunning, Morrison, and Stephen were just about the only ones left in Allegheny. Henry already had a house of his own; Ann Eliza and her husband and children had gone to Olney, Pennsylvania, to live. Henrietta had so many children of her own to look after that she had little time for anything else.

So Stephen, Morrison, Henry, and the others agreed to sell the Allegheny house, and Stephen and Jane at last moved into a home of their own. Jane liked being away from her inlaws, and it was quieter for Stephen, too. He seemed a little happier for a while, and he seemed to have more energy.

He worked hard enough—with poor results. Only one or two songs in a year, and those songs weren't up to his others. He began to borrow money again. He owed rent on the house. He wrote to his publishers to see if there was any money in his account. They told him they had already given him money in advance, and there was nothing due him.

"Your songs aren't selling very well lately," they told him. "Why don't you write us another one like 'My Old Kentucky Home' or 'Jeanie with the Light Brown Hair'?"

Stephen had so many debts that Firth, Pond & Co. agreed to pay him everything they thought his songs that he had already written would ever earn. They sent him a check for $1,872.28, and Stephen signed a new contract with them. The contract said that he no longer owned the songs he had written so far. Firth, Pond owned them, and they would take a chance on being able to sell them to earn the money they were paying Stephen Foster.

With almost two thousand dollars Stephen was able to pay his rent and debts and buy clothes for Jane and Marian. But if he wanted any more money, he would have to write new songs.

His brothers urged him to write Negro songs, since everybody seemed to be talking more and more about slavery. Newspapers wrote about slavery; politicians made speeches about it. The abolitionists wanted slavery abolished altogether and the slaves set free. Others approved of slavery.

When slaves escaped from the Far South and told of their sufferings, people became more excited about slavery.

There were no slaves in Pennsylvania where the Fosters lived. Pennsylvania was a free state. Lieve had not been a slave but a maid who worked in the Foster household when Stephen was a baby.

Stephen's brothers were interested in politics, but Stephen was not. He didn't feel strong enough to argue and wrangle, and if he became excited his cough would start right up.

Stephen Foster was a kindly, gentle person who did not like to know that anyone suffered. He wanted to see slavery ended and the slaves set free. He thought about all the Negroes he had ever known—Lieve, the dock men, and one other in particular. He thought of the one who had worked in Jane's home when Stephen was courting her.

His name had been Joe. He had done all manner of odd jobs around the house, and he drove the buggy for Jane's family. He walked around the house dressed up in a long-tailed blue coat with shining brass buttons. Whenever Stephen called with his bouquet of flowers to see Jane, Joe would open the door for him and bow low.

"Miss Jenny," Joe would call. "You have a visitor."

Those had been happy days, Stephen thought. Jane had had many more things in her father's house before she married Stephen Foster. She had had pretty dresses, lovely furniture, and servants.

Stephen ran his fingers over the piano keys and remembered Joe—Old Black Joe. He began to think of a new melody with words about Joe and the good old days.

"Gone are the days when my heart was young and gay," Stephen wrote.

That was true of him as well as Joe. *His* good old days were gone, too.

He worked long and hard over the song. At last he had it finished.

> "I'm coming, I'm coming,
> For my head is bending low;
> I hear those gentle voices calling,
> 'Old Black Joe.'"

Jane cried when he played it and sang it for her. She remembered Old Black Joe. Joe had looked after her all the time she was growing up. He had taken her driving in the buggy. He had answered the door for her gentlemen friends when she was a young lady.

Of course, the song was a success. "Old Black Joe" was as popular as "My Old Kentucky Home."

The song gave Stephen back his self-confidence.

He felt hopeful and happy again. His discouragement vanished. Jane felt happy, too. Perhaps her Stephen would settle down to hard work and write a whole list of successful songs.

Maybe he had just been lonesome these last few years. His mother and father were dead; some of his brothers and sisters had moved away. He probably missed them. Now that Stephen was feeling better, why not move to another city where he could make new friends? Why not move to New York where his publisher was located?

Stephen and Jane talked it over.

"Moving to New York seems like a good idea," they agreed.

So they packed up their things, took their daughter, Marian, and traveled East.

SICK AND ALONE

CHAPTER
12

NEW YORK CITY WAS A happy place for a while. Stephen was gay. He and Jane went about meeting interesting people—other composers, singers, musicians. Jane had a new silk gown, and Stephen wore a blue swallow-tailed coat with a high silk hat.

They went to parties, too, and one evening when they were preparing for a masquerade ball, Stephen announced that he had plans of his own. Jane felt a little frightened, because sometimes she wondered if Stephen was being too gay.

"I'll be along later," said Stephen. "I am going to surprise all of you."

Jane put on her costume and went along with their friends, and Stephen didn't tell her what disguise he was going to wear. Jane was worried. She searched through the crowd for Stephen all evening, afraid that his old sickness, his chills and fevers, his cough, might be overcoming him again. She didn't find him until the dancing was over and the guests were having refreshments. There was Stephen! In the orchestra, playing a violin and wearing false whiskers. His disguise was the most successful, because no one had recognized him. No one thought of looking in the orchestra for him.

But Jane knew that Stephen was really wasting away as she watched his flushed and feverish face. He probably had tuberculosis, but in those days doctors didn't understand the ailment. They didn't know that Stephen should stay in bed in a healthful sanitarium until he was cured. Instead, he went right on composing songs, going to parties, having chills and fever, sometimes having coughing spells.

He wrote a whole list of songs during their first year in New York, but they didn't sell many copies. They were shallow songs, written in too much of a hurry, and not as beautiful and as full of feeling as "Old Black Joe."

Money didn't come in fast enough to support Stephen and Jane. Stephen wrote to Morrison for help, and Morrison sent what money he could. Firth, Pond & Co. began to lose patience with Stephen. He wasn't writing as many songs as he promised. They had once more sent him money in advance, and he owed them almost fifteen hundred dollars.

Jane's and Stephen's clothes began to look threadbare, and they had to stop going to parties. Jane pressed and mended and repaired and did what she could to keep up appearances. She was becoming discouraged again. Sometimes she and Stephen quarreled.

"Think of the baby, Stephen," Jane would plead. "She's old enough to go to school."

But the sicker Stephen became, the more difficult and unreasonable he grew. At last Jane became so discouraged and so worried that she took their daughter, Marian, and went to Pennsylvania to live with her sister. Jane wanted to look after Stephen, but she had to look after her daughter, too.

Confused and alone, Stephen Foster wandered through the streets of New York, not noticing the crowds that milled about and jostled and pushed him. The crowds shouted and talked politics. Lincoln had been elected president in 1860, and the people of the United States were more excited than ever about slavery. Some Southern states said they were going to leave the United States altogether. Soon several Southern states had seceded from the Union and held a meeting to form their own government. They called themselves the Confederate States of America. The Civil War was starting!

There were big meetings right in the street, men shouting about joining the army. They didn't notice the lonely, thin man walking along— Stephen Foster in ragged clothes and worn-out shoes, keeping close to the buildings, holding his coat closed against the cold air. He paid no attention to the speeches and shoutings.

Jane came back to New York to see Stephen once or twice, each time finding him worse off.

"Stephen," she would say. "Please come back to Pennsylvania so that your family can look after you."

He wouldn't go.

He was really too sick to know what he wanted to do. He was smoking too many cigarettes. He was even drinking.

"Stephen," Jane would plead. "Please don't drink. It isn't good for you."

Stephen was too depressed and discouraged to listen to anyone. When one of his brothers came to New York to see him, he paid no attention to what was said. His whole family was worried about him.

He was trying to write any kind of songs that his publisher would buy. He composed a few war songs, but war wasn't Stephen's favorite subject. He didn't like violence.

He found a cheap place to live in the Bowery, in a hotel where other writers lived because they couldn't afford to pay very much rent. The Bowery was really a gathering place for ragged ne'er-do-wells. Stephen became so ragged and poor that he looked just like any other vagabond.

Every day he used to visit the back room of a grocery and liquor store, where he sat at one of the tables to write. If he couldn't afford music paper, he would write on a piece of brown wrapping paper. He drank homemade rum that the store-keeper kept in a small barrel nearby, and more often than not he forgot to eat. If he felt hungry at all, he would take an apple or a piece of raw turnip from the vegetable stand.

Tired of sitting in the grocery store, discouraged at not being able to think of a new melody, he would wander out into the street.

Stephen happened into a music store one day. The storekeeper in the back of the room who knew Stephen watched him come through the door. He laughed and said,

"Steve looks down and out."

The girl waiting on the counter was startled. She had heard of Stephen Foster, had sold his songs over that counter many times.

"Is this Mr. Foster?" she asked timidly, walking toward the visitor.

"Yes," replied the untidy man. "The wreck of Stephen Foster."

"Oh, no!" said the young lady. "I feel it an honor to take by the hand the writer of 'Old Folks at Home.' "

Stephen's eyes filled with tears.

"You have spoken the first kind words I have heard in a long time," he told her.

In spite of his rags and untidy appearance, anyone who talked to him could tell that he was a man of culture. His voice was gentle and his language was scholarly. He was only thirty-seven years old, but he seemed much older because of his illness.

After he had talked to the girl for a while, he drifted away from the music store—probably back to the table in the back of the grocery store.

Stephen Foster lived on in poverty. He was writing any kind of songs and selling them to anybody who would buy them. He no longer had a contract with Firth, Pond & Co. He wasn't writing Negro songs any more. The songs he did write were not good, although he was writing a lot of them. The publishers who bought them paid him very little.

STEPHEN FOSTER'S
LAST SONG

CHAPTER

13

N A JANUARY EVE-
ning in 1864 Stephen
Foster came home, cold and tired, to his bleak little
room. He had walked too far, and his thin coat
had not been protection enough against the sharp
air. He was shivering inside.

In order to get warm he undressed and slid into
bed, drawing the bedclothes up around his chin,
and as the chills faded away, he relaxed and soon
dropped off to sleep.

During the night he awoke feeling very thirsty,
and he started out of bed to pour himself a glass of
water. He was so weak and faint that he stumbled
and fell forward against the table, sending the water
pitcher and wash basin crashing to the floor, covering the carpet with sharp-edged pieces.

Stephen crashed down on top of the broken fragments, cutting his face and neck. Too weak to help himself up, he lay there on the floor for the rest of the night.

When the maid came in the next morning to fix his room, she found him still on the floor, bleeding and suffering. Excited and shocked, not knowing just what to do, she hurried out and told one of his friends, a Mr. George Cooper.

A few minutes later Mr. Cooper rushed in and knelt beside the man on the floor, feeling his pulse and his forehead.

All Stephen could do was to lift his head and gasp, "I'm done for."

Mr. Cooper realized that Stephen's condition was serious, so he helped him into a carriage and took him to Bellevue Hospital. Then he wrote to Stephen's brother, Morrison:

"Your brother Stephen I am sorry to inform you is lying in Bellevue Hospital in this city very sick. Can you send him some money, since his means are very low. If possible, he would like to see you in person."

Stephen Foster just lay in bed with his eyes closed, while the nurse bathed his wounds. He lay still all night, dozing fitfully.

The next day he was able to sit up with pillows at his back. He seemed more cheerful, and nobody realized how sick he was. The nurse came in to change his bandages, and as she stood beside his bed, Stephen fainted.

That was the end. In a few hours he was dead—before any of his family could reach New York to be with him.

The doctors at the hospital knew the patient's name was Foster, but they didn't realize that he was the famous Stephen Foster. They thought he was just another vagabond from the Bowery, and so they sent his body to the city morgue. George Cooper had to hurry to the morgue and explain the mistake.

When Stephen's sisters and brothers and wife, Jane, came to the city, they arranged for a proper funeral, taking Stephen home to be buried in Allegheny Cemetery, beside his mother and father.

Stephen Foster left little: a few worn clothes and his purse. In his purse were a few cents and a scrap of paper, on which he had scribbled an idea for a new song, "Dear Friends and Gentle Hearts—" Stephen had died before he could write the song.

When his brothers visited Stephen's hotel room, they found his notebook, the one in which he had written many of his songs. They leafed through the pages. There was "Way Down upon the Swanee River." They saw where he had crossed out the words Pee Dee River and changed them to Swanee River. There was "Oh! doo-dah-day!" and "Jeanie with the Light Brown Hair," and "Old Black Joe" all written in Stephen's own hand.

On one of the last pages in the notebook they came across a song they had never heard. It was called "Beautiful Dreamer."

"Beautiful dreamer, queen of my song,
List while I woo thee with soft melody.
Gone are the cares of life's busy throng,
Beautiful dreamer, awake unto me!"

Some think it is the last song Stephen Foster ever wrote. No one is certain. Whenever he wrote it, "Beautiful Dreamer" was published a few weeks after he died, and the world had one more masterpiece by the talented Stephen Foster.

The Foster songs which people remember and sing today are his finest. They are American folk songs, and they are beautiful music.

Stephen Foster is one of America's greatest composers.